The Mandala : Coloring Book for Adult

Alin J.

Mandala : Coloring for Stress Relief

Copyright: Published in the United States by Alin J.
Published October 2016

ISBN-13:978-1539701927

ISBN-10:1539701921

www.ingramcontent.com/pod-product-compliance
Lightning Source LLC
Chambersburg PA
CBHW051947280526
45789CB00009B/3194